Dearest Workman family,
What a blessing not only to be such great friends but family as well. Your support of my book means everything to me!

Love you all
Jeanine
aka
"Ruthie"

Ruthie Jo Wilson

"It's Not Going to Be Easy."
GOD

A Memoir

WESTBOW
PRESS
A DIVISION OF THOMAS NELSON
& ZONDERVAN

Copyright © 2015 Ruthie Jo Wilson.

All rights reserved. No part of this book may be used or reproduced by any means, graphic, electronic, or mechanical, including photocopying, recording, taping or by any information storage retrieval system without the written permission of the publisher except in the case of brief quotations embodied in critical articles and reviews.

WestBow Press books may be ordered through booksellers or by contacting:

WestBow Press
A Division of Thomas Nelson & Zondervan
1663 Liberty Drive
Bloomington, IN 47403
www.westbowpress.com
1 (866) 928-1240

Because of the dynamic nature of the Internet, any web addresses or links contained in this book may have changed since publication and may no longer be valid. The views expressed in this work are solely those of the author and do not necessarily reflect the views of the publisher, and the publisher hereby disclaims any responsibility for them.

Any people depicted in stock imagery provided by Thinkstock are models, and such images are being used for illustrative purposes only. Certain stock imagery © Thinkstock.

ISBN: 978-1-4908-8071-6 (sc)
ISBN: 978-1-4908-8070-9 (e)

Library of Congress Control Number: 2015907500

Print information available on the last page.

WestBow Press rev. date: 05/20/2015

Contents

The Beginning of the End 1

"It's Not Going to be Easy." God 4

January 2013: Refinement and Sorrow 10

Changing Heart 17

Choices 26

Spiritual Warfare 2013 33

Peace in Heartbreak 38

Closing Doors 51

Starting Over 64

Beautiful Ugly 72

The Beginning of the End

I remember precisely the conversational exchange I had with my Lord and Savior. I was alone in my thoughts while I was driving along on a hilly, lonely stretch of highway. It was a sunny, chilly 'happy' day. However, my heart was broken and hurt. I was disgusted and ashamed of myself. I had a sinking feeling; "What kind of person would I be today had I been more diligent about the commitment to my faith in Christ Jesus?" That awakening in my broken spirit instantly charged my heart into a firm commitment of determination. My heart had finally caught up to the knowledge and what it meant to be completely surrendered to Christ Jesus. At that precise moment, I knew that I had come to the end of my worldly behavior. It was the beginning of the end for me. It was at that profound, pivotal moment that I would commit myself to the life God had intended for me. The living word of the Bible penetrated my soul; my heart was open to receive the Holy Spirit's prompting and my ears were finally open to listen. It would be months later that I was able to understand the transformation that had happened to me. At that moment of heartfelt surrender, the words of the Bible began to live in me.

> "I have been crucified with Christ; and it is no longer I who live, but
> Christ lives in me; and the life which I now live in the flesh I live by
> Faith in the Son of God, who loved me,
> And delivered Himself up for me."
> Galatians 2:20
> The New American Standard Bible

I passionately write this memoir because I know that there are people like me who hurt deeply. I would wake up most mornings rehearsing the same agonizing voice in my head about how much of a failure I was; that I had no real significance in life and decided

"It's Not Going to Be Easy." God

that the world would be a better place without me. Yet somewhere deep inside of my soul something told me that those horrid thoughts just couldn't be true. Year after year I used different remedies to smother those self-defeating voices in my head. So often I lived life weighted down with 'damage control' because of the poor decisions I created for myself. Oddly enough, the cure and remedy for me was in me through God my Creator. And as perfect timing would lend itself, a family member told me directly, "I promise you will be transformed if you give yourself over to God the Father." For the first time in my life I trusted what he said and His promise to be Truth.

"It's Not Going to be Easy." God

On that long rural highway that I was traveling on, I began to reflect on my life. I wondered what poor personal choices could have been thwarted had I centered myself on my God who created me and is my Personal Savior. What kind of person would I be today had I applied myself to the solidity truth based on the living words of the Holy Bible? What path of my life would have been different had I become a committed, attentive student through Biblical teachings? Which of my prayers and questions would have been answered accurately had I stopped running from personal issues? What infinite wisdom from the Lord had I missed because of the 'motor' that drove me away from facing past mistakes? How many days of my life would I have enjoyed more had I allowed the Lord to bestow upon me peace; patience;

quietness and gentleness? God began to renew my mind in a profound way; my 'blinded' eyes were open and my 'silenced' ears were alert. One day I read a portion of a popular Christian devotional book. The Lord affirmed the alignment of what He wanted for me:

> "I am leading you along a way that is uniquely right for you. The closer to Me you grow, the more fully you become your true self- the one I designed you to be."
>
> The New American Standard Bible

I had made choices in my life that were apart from God; as if I was arrogant enough to believe I could do a better job than God, my Creator. I visualized myself free-falling into the arms of Jesus who enables all of creation with hope and strength. My life had been diving into several dark paths by making choices absent from God. Instead, I desired my life to be thriving in the rich blessings of a close walk with the Lord Jesus Christ.

I became a believer at the age of thirteen. I began to recognize the futility of my life, for all those years, apart from the Lord to the current crisis I was in at the moment. I had let the bondage of fear, mistrust, anger, depression and a poor self-image absorb my thoughts and penetrate my heart. I had carried out my heart issues in outrageous behaviors unrecognized by other believers. I had contorted my life apart from God because of the 'death-grip' I had on those miserable and unhealthy issues. It was the only way I had known to survive, yet if this was survival I was ready to let go. It was time to allow God to begin to pry my 'fingers' off those unhealthy issues that had created a chain of bondage for so many years.

I acknowledged the bondage in my life and I **outwardly** voiced to my Savior:

"Lord, I have had enough of my life. I am done. You said that there is a life laid out before me that is so rich with blessings it is incomprehensible to the human mind. I want that life. I want that life free from all the weight and bondage in my life. All of it. I want You to heal everything in my life. All of it."

"It's Not Going to Be Easy." God

And I firmly believed He could and would.

I 'heard' the Lord. I know I did. Deep within my ears, I heard God audibly and distinctly in my heart. There was no doubt that the Lord answered me.

"Are you sure? Are you ready?"

I answered aloud,

"Yes, I don't care what it takes."

Again, I heard the Lord say:

"Ok. But it is not going to be easy".

Again, audibly I said:

"I don't care I am ready".

And I meant it.

The intimacy with Christ was so strong and the words I spoke so clearly to Him rang out more confidence than I had been my whole life. By rediscovering the Bible I see now that the Lord and I together were living out the verse:

> "For I know the plans that I have for you," declares the LORD, 'plans for welfare and not for calamity to give you a future and a hope." Jeremiah 29:11
>
> The New American Standard Bible

I had heard and read Bible verses throughout the years. But in that precise moment, the words; "For I know the plans that I have for you ." resonated every part of me. Physically, I was feeling less stressed and more relaxed. Mentally, I felt peaceful and strong. Spiritually, I was scared but I knew that there was no turning back this time. I pressed forward like the vehicle I was driving. Not only was I moving onward, I had turned my back to the former ways of my turbulent life. Through blind faith, I knew that anything was better than the life I had lead so far and presently where my life was leading me to. Furthermore, there was no one on earth that could have removed the complications of my world strive and dissatisfaction. Year after year, I was searching for a secret formula only to discover that Christ is the perfect Counselor leading me in the right direction. His words from the Bible are the perfect self-help book. His parables are the perfect sermon of leadership and encouragement. Christ is the best parent and best friend because of His unconditional love. I was looking forward to my new life that would be richly blessed as Christ has promised.

Naturally I was processing so much at that moment of surrender. After all it was a profound life altering moment to say the least! Logically, anything was better than the life I was living. And clearly if God created us in His image, His love was way above my human understanding. I began to think of God as not only the Creator of the Heaven and the Earth but that He created me, knowing me intimately. If my God has the power to create the universe then that same God has a personal interested in me. Knowing the history of the Bible, He wanted us to live in a perfect place on earth. But because of sin, we live in a fallen world carried on by generation after generation. There is nothing that would ever dissolve how God really feels about His creation including me. We are and I am so carefully constructed; higher than any living thing on earth; unexplainable marvel of our intricate design. Why would the creator be such a perfectionist if he did not love me? My curious nature wanted to know that intimate life with Him and what it could be for my future.

January 2013: Refinement and Sorrow

The Lord stated very clearly to me that my decision to surrender to Him was 'not going to be easy'. I knew that I was in for something different this time. I had developed a running 'tape deck' in my mind throughout the years. One train of thought was that I could lose my salvation. And because I had never felt 'good enough' I decided to just run with the world. (That transformative thought process is to question whether my choices are beneficial to those around me or not. I know that I can be in the world but not of the world'. ['Do not love the world, nor the things in the world. If anyone loves the world, the love of the Father is not in him.' I John 2:15]).

The second thought was that everything that I wanted I demanded that I get it through

"It's Not Going to Be Easy." God

prayer. I had created my own demons of frustration, poutiness and self-pity when God didn't answer my prayers. I had created a 'stop and go' relationship with Christ. For example, I thought it was great and wonderful when He answered my prayer. So began a short-term zealous attitude around my faith. However, in protest and in contrast I would question, "God, why didn't you answer my prayer?" In self-pity, I would stomp away in a torrent of frustrated faith. Under conviction one day I thought, "Just call me Israel. Time after time I've cried to You, Lord. You answered my prayers in miraculous ways only for me to forget". I would end up in yet another 'ditch' crying out again for a way out. But that moment on the highway with a genuine surrender made things different. My "Yo- Yo" faith was gone. There was no longer any more up- and -down belief toward God.

> *"For My thoughts are not your thoughts, neither are your ways My ways," declares the Lord." Isaiah 55:8*
> The New American Standard Bible

What I did not know is that my renewed commitment to God meant a season of extreme and intense refinery.

> "And some of those who have insight will fall, in order to refine, purge and make them pure....." Daniel 11:35a
> The New American Standard Bible

Simultaneously, I sensed that my 30+ year old marriage was dessinagrating rapidly. The veil from my eyes was beginning to lift and I suddenly became painfully aware of the toll that we had both put on our marriage. My husband, Samuel, was dealing with years of suppression from a painful past in combination with years of our struggling marriage. I had suddenly realized that I had taken advantage of the continual, mainstream of unconditional love that Samuel had poured out to me for years. In addition, I had allowed a self-inflicted, manipulative way of emotionally disablement placed on Sam. I received all his efforts of love and support yet I had rarely reciprocated that support to him. Naturally and eventually this relational exchange had given way to a flood of strain, stress and pressure. Meanwhile, his job was in crisis with irreversible consequences.

God had designed my inner nature with a very sensitive and tender spirit. Furthermore, I was meant to walk in God's light because the conviction of the Holy Spirit was heavily and powerfully upon me. The shame that I continued to feel was so weary. The pattern that I always took in the past was to console myself by walking in darkness. I did not know this at the time but 'refinery' was necessary for my future but it was an excruciating painful process. My relationship with my soul-mate was nearly severed. I did not handle the refinement and the absence of a healthy marriage well at all. I had known the Bible verse:

> "Be anxious for nothing, but in everything by prayer
> And supplication with thanksgiving let your requests
> Be made known to God." Philippians 4:6
> The New American Standard Bible

However, I did not apply this Bible verse that God had prescribed for me. Anxiousness became an idol because I was so focused primarily on our marital problem. I ignored or made a small attempt to validate this command from God. And it was to my detriment. It could have served as a layer of protection while I was going through such tough refinery. Our Father has instructions for all situations. This includes applications to protect us from life's adversities, consequences, crisis and the purification process. I was in a constant state of anxiety and turmoil. Many times I panicked and overacted emotionally. I have concluded that this constant state of mental tension caused physical muscle pain. That is why the Lord had commissioned me to: "Be anxious for nothing...."

However, I had received assurance that it was ok for me to grieve. It showed that I cared enough to feel sorrow for the situation. It was also an oath that my own personal anguish would not last forever.

"It's Not Going to Be Easy." God

"A time to weep, and a time to laugh;
A time to mourn and a time to dance."
Ecclesiastes 3: 4
 The New American Standard Bible

So despondent, I would cry myself to sleep. I was hardly functioning and I stopped taking care of myself hygienically. I would often wake up late for work and wouldn't bother washing my face or washing my hair. Once at work, I bombarded and burdened my coworkers constantly and continually. (Something I completely regret. It was unfair to drag my dear friends into my sadness). I would cry so hard at times that I wouldn't be able to swallow causing secondary symptoms of panic. There were many days that I was convinced that my heart would finally give out because it was so grieved and broken. My very active lifestyle, including my love for outdoor exercising had come to an end. Instead I would curl up in bed repeating and rehearsing the Lord's Prayer. I would ask My Father to cover me in His blanket and I would feel His warm, peaceful presence over me. My relationship and my friendship with Jesus Christ became very endearing and very sweet. One evening, I found enough strength to go to a Christian Based Recovery Program. After the service, I sheepishly walked forward into the arms of a Christian sister for a hug and a prayer. Suddenly, I was aware and embarrassed over my appearance! I had been wearing very baggy, loose jogging pants; a huge sweat-shirt that was colossal on my small framed body; my grubby hair was scruffily thrown up in a bun and my grimy unwashed face was covered in tear stains. I felt mortified with myself. But yet again, I heard Jesus reassure me by a clear whisper:

"It's okay. You don't feel well."

Changing Heart

I have often sensed that there had been no transitions from my birth to the membership of our family church growing up in Michigan! I felt like I was born and raised there! And generally speaking, I was. I kept a worn out bulletin from my church called Kentwood Church of Christ. It was dated September 30, 1962 and typed in it was:

"BUNDLE FROM HEAVEN

Everyone is happy at the Rick Johnson home! Mrs. Ellen Johnson finally gave birth last Monday to a ten-pound baby girl."

I have very strong memories of my upbringing in that church. A powerful impact and my fondest memories are singing as a congregation from the traditional church hymnals! I so loved everything about the composition of those songs. I was not a scholarly student academically but for music, I learned quickly and still hold its understanding. I took piano lessons from the pastor's wife and she taught me about compositions, melodies and harmonies. I was able to identify musical bars, scales, notes and beats; the force of *forte* and the briefness of *staccato*. I would read the biography of the composer, how the song was inspired and what year it went to print. Those sweet and powerful musical words are fossilized on my heart and in my mind. There is no greater joy for me to able to sing with a church that still references the old traditional church hymnals.

As a young church going family, little subtle incidences began to chip away at our desire and commitment to the church. But worse than that, we were blind to the tiny temptations seeping into our family which would ultimately grow into some destructive behavior. Music didn't destroy us but it was absent from our home that would have provided a way to acknowledge our Lord and worship the Supreme Deity of this world.

There came a time in my church attendance that I became very opinionated, uncomfortable and oppositional to the new contemporary Christian songs that were being transitioned in churches all over the country. I suppose in part because I was a stamped as a church traditionalist. But no matter, for a short while I could not relate to the worship aspect of Contemporary Christian Music. However, when the Lord prompted me to connect my mind with my heart and had determined to surrender myself to the Lord, my spirit began to change. It had been a transformation that I had not controlled nor forced. I knew that I was not the one who altered my heart to automatically tune in to Contemporary Christian music. All of a sudden, I had a deep desire to begin listening and worshipping our Father through Contemporary Christian music. This new renovation of my heart caused my ears to listen differently. This particular lesson was clear; I did not need to be in control of everything. I could benefit from God doing all the work! This immense miracle showed me how I could live in correlation with a Christ centered life and give up the exhausting struggle to dominate my life.

I had changed within the change. My first love of music was Traditional Hymnals. Instantly, I had begun to listen to all forms of Contemporary Christian music. At times, my heart was so broken I listened to gentle subdued and serious Christian songs. Those particular songs empathized with my grief and I had sensed that the artists' knew what I was going through. Those songs had given me reprieve from the sorrow; had lifted me up with a morsel of hope and provided a message that I could get up-and-get moving on. Not only was I singing Christian songs for the first time but it became an act of worship alone in my car and in my home!

I was beginning to understand the Christian experience of worshipping and praise with song. My daughter and son-in-law were active with this experience at their church. I purchased tickets to a city wide Christian Music Festival with my family in mind. It was a gift to them and I knew they would enjoy the event. They were unable to go. I was disappointed and I never considered going to the event. I tried to give the tickets away or even sell them to no avail. Samuel and I were at odds the day of the festival so I huffed and puffed all the way there by myself. The Lord ordained that time alone for me to focus on Him. The gathering was at a massive outdoor venue. Hot from the weather and the long walk, I felt downtrodden. I plopped into a seat as far as I could get away from people and the center-stage.

I was predetermined to get some use from the tickets and stay for just an hour or two. I could clearly hear each high profile artist give their heartfelt testimony to the masses but also directly to me. It appeared as if each one of their messages carried a common theme; there had been a season of refinery after struggles and difficulties in their life. The Lord had made it clear that their lives would change in a powerful way; that the Lord would predetermine their future in such a way that no human intellect could ever understand. Most of the artists agreed that what they were doing currently was something they could have never absorbed had they been told ahead of time.

Is this not so typical of God the Creator?! I concluded that if one is to be used by God in a mighty way, He alone has to prepare His people for His glory. In the grand scheme of creation, isn't this appropriate? The Christian walk is a precept of discipline. Through the conviction of the Holy Spirit, I began to understand that I too needed to be set apart, refined and disciplined before I am able to be used for God's glory. One morning as I was reading the Old Testament of the Bible, God the Creator allowed for me to understand an intensely, overwhelming and overpowering connection between the Creation of the Universe to me as an individual. Ultimately, God will prepare the world to gaze upon His Power and Glory through the chosen, set-apart Nation of Israel. The Nation of Israel had to have its residence purified through God's refinery before the Country of Israel could be established. Again, in due course, all humans will fix their eyes upon God's chosen Nation of Israel. Presently, every country surrounding the topography of Israel is under turmoil. It is hard

"It's Not Going to Be Easy." God

to ignore the increasing horrific; turbulent; hostile; impure; and unrest streaming through different avenues of the news. Because God cannot gaze upon anything impure, He has a protective layering upon Israel. I claimed this awareness to be applied to my life and to my heart.

God had a hold of me at that Christian Festival. I became absorbed, captivated, mesmerized and enthralled. I felt adhesive in my little sacred spot for over 7 hours. My very active internal momentum had come to a stop. This was from my Powerful God and not of my doing. I was being deeply ministered to by my Almighty God alone among the mass of people time and space. I felt a strong peaceful, safe presence from the Holy Spirit. In a twinkle of an eye, I sensed a reality and vision of what heaven would be like. With that in mind, I also realized I was feeling no fear, mourning, distress and no physical aches and pains. The faraway and isolated bright lights permeated the dark evening with a serene calm. The heat of the day began to diffuse by the setting of the sun and a cool, gentle breeze was released to the arena.

The songs, praise and worship infiltrated and continually filled the night air. The words of the song were displayed on a giant screen giving an even deeper eternal meaning. There was a constant stream of unending music; words; praising and worshipping to a God full of love. I felt cherished, treasured, valued and complete.

The event began to wind down. The last musicians were saying their good-byes and well wishes. People were beginning to stir and were leaving their seats. The blaring lights began to shine back onto reality. Time had stopped for me. I could have stayed in that very spot for eternity. I had just been a part of something that I could never adequately portray in words. That something was so spiritual and Godly. Every fiber of my being had witnessed the Power of God. All of sudden I realized that all my worldly struggles were nonexistent for that stretch of time in worship. I had finally felt how God the Creator of the Universe loved me just as I am. I sang and wept tears of joy and experienced peace. My heart could have burst from a flowing of praise and worship. The event had had composed a new spirit in me.

When I left from 'my spot', I had to check my heart to make sure I was not walking away with a superficial 'spiritual high'. I had done this so often after a large Christian event. That 'high' would eventually wear away, thrusting me into another disappointment. I felt different and was not looking for that miraculous 'wand' that had the ability to whisk away all my problems in a blink. It was late so I petitioned for a ride home. I walked into the parking lot of reality; however this encounter with God strengthened me in an eternal way...

> "to *obtain* an inheritance *which* is imperishable and undefiled and will not fade away, reserved in heaven for you," 1 Peter 1:4
> The New American Standard Bible

Choices

I became a believer of Jesus Christ as a young teenager. My Heavenly Father has been close to my side ever since I became a child of God. He led me to Samuel in 1981. We shared a very strong connection and I believed he was my soul-mate. Sam and I were married in 1983. I was a confused Christian raised in believing I could lose my faith. Because of my wedding promises made to God, I considered myself in the 'safe zone' of life. I was done (temporarily) carousing with the world. I once again, resurrected my zealous faith with the Lord and strongly encouraged my husband to attend church with our brand new baby. Thankful to the Lord, Samuel had a miraculously and radical conversion when he walked forward after the sermon had been delivered one Sunday. We began to conduct our brand new faith and commitment to Christ in a very dramatic sense. We had been acquainted with the Christian life and knew the importance of guiding our young children with the foundation of Jesus Christ. We had begun to anchor ourselves on the promises of our Lord. Yet, we had not fully grasped the daily discipline and the assurance to walk in faith. We had not fully comprehended that Jesus was sent as our Savior; that the Son of God was chosen to be the sacrificial lamb that took upon the sins of the world. Jesus died a brutal death so that believers, such as Samuel and I could live an abundant life beyond anything we could envision.

A few years into our Christian marriage, we became more focused on the perks and benefits of Christian living. We somehow believed that we could scathe by in ease, conducting our decisions in a fallen world. Living life in a worldly sense is relatively easy compared to joining the Spiritual Battle of God's Army. We had not applied the critical verse from 2 Corinthians 12:9b:

> "...My grace is sufficient for you, for power is perfected in weakness..."

We were miraculously blessed beyond any human comprehension with materialistic items, yet continued to forget about what the Lord had done for us. We became engulfed in our disappointments from other Christians.

Our marriage was full of self-inflicted problems. Its compass was not always centered and gauged to look north to Jesus as our Savior. Instead, our marriage was a shaky as a ship being tossed around in the ocean. We had heart issues and our treasures were not necessarily focused on the life guided by God's path. Somehow we believed that God would continue and miraculously take care of our foolish spending habits and decision making apart from Him. We took our eyes off of our dependence on Christ and began to create our own 'idols.' We had ignored the warnings of the dangers that were ebbing a way at our relationship and figured God would keep us covered from the attacks of our marriage. What we didn't realize is that we were two individuals joined as one with unresolved issues from a troubled past. Our new Christian commitment was used loosely to cover deep wounds.

I often look back at the years we paved for ourselves. The harsh reality is that we cannot go back to the past to remedy our mistakes. However, my hope and dream is to help strengthen Christians in their walk with Christ. My desire is to look back to move forward with greater resolve. I now know how serious the commitment to our Heavenly Father is for a healthy, thriving marriage.

I know that God used our passionate personalities in several beneficial ways but unchecked, we muddled the clear line and direction God had planned for our marriage. Our Yo-Yo faith caused a lot of unnecessary pain and hurt.

> '"So because you are lukewarm, and neither hot nor cold, I will spit you out of My mouth. " Revelation 3:16
> The New American Standard Bible

There were many seasons of our marriage that we headed downward only to crawl our way back from the depths we had put ourselves in. I now find it necessary to build a strong foundation on the truth of God's word so that when tough times approach it will sustain a marriage. I am just recalculating that perhaps new Christian marriages could possibly start with systematic 'baby-steps'. Our service to the church was beneficial in so many ways. But perhaps our over-zealous desires skimmed over the essential processes to grow onward to Christ likeness. Perceivably, mastering the 'crawling' stage together in the Christian faith would have served to strengthen us for the baby-steps; to provide a slow, upward movement to a strong upright Christian 'walk'. We most definitely gunned- out-of-the-gate passing the opportunity to walk along side with other Christians! Additionally, we dashed past the base of the Cross where we could have daily placed and released our misguidances. This is the same Cross of Jesus where we can lay down and liberate the bondage of flesh and selfishness.

For me personally, I look at Jesus' Cross differently. I can visualize Christ with His outstretched hands of support and encouragement. All of my life, I ran away from those arms. In fear, I took off in a full sprint, head-strong in my own direction. There have been so many walls that would knock me down. But just like a child, I dusted myself off and continued on my own destructive path. Finally, I hit 'the wall' hard enough that it really hurt. I made the choice to have My Savior pick me up and dust me off. I finally fell into His loving arms, sobbing from all the bruises in my life. Now I want to live my life that will help people in His way. I do not want to miss out on those gifts He gave me to open and share while on this earth. Because I am a believer in God the Father; Jesus Christ, His only Son and the Holy Spirit who is with us always, I am assured a place in heaven. But I want to know His way of being more effective living a Spirit Filled Life. I would like for Him to equip me to help this world that is becoming more and more challenging. I want to get healthy and strong to swim against the tide from the raging seas of this world. I want to use my suffering to encourage others not settle into the skewed –norms of life.

Spiritual Warfare 2013

On New Year's Eve 2012, I decided to do some art work. I painted a "Welcome 2013" sign to be placed in my front entry way. An unexpected dread came over me on the spot and I knew it was not going to be a good year. My surrendered experience to the Lord had only been weeks before the start of 2013. I had reached out to a Pastor on one very oppressive day. He instructed me that an essential, critical and targetable objective for a believer in God is to:

1. Have an open and active communication with our Heavenly Father through **Prayer.** This forms the ability to ask God for our needs and worship His deity.

    Pray without ceasing. 1 Thessalonians 5:17

2. Immerse oneself to the powerful living words of the **Bible** to bring about: conviction, inspiration, wisdom, salvation and service. And to ultimately receive messages on conducting our life.

> For the word of God is living and active and sharper than any two-edged sword, and piercing as far as the division of soul and spirit, of both joints and marrow, and able to judge the thoughts and intentions of the heart. Hebrews 4:12
> The New American Standard Bible

3. **Congregate** with a part of a body of believers. The pastor knew that if Christians were to converge with each other that a large portion of our human needs would be satisfied by ministering to others. Assembling, gathering and congregating would empower means of accountability and support.

"It's Not Going to Be Easy." God

Not forsaking our own assembling together, as is the habit of some, but encouraging *one another*; and all the more, as you see the day drawing near. Hebrews 10:25
The New American Standard Bible

I understood these fundamentals of the Christian life. But astonishing, inconceivable, extraordinary power came to my existence when this knowledge infiltrated and infused my heart. By handling the management of my unsettled, tumultuous life I inadvertently created brazen idols. I had been 'glancing' up to God. I had been giving the Creator fleeting and momentary glimpses. My life was not fixated, absorbed, occupied, immersed and gripped by God. But now my heart was changed. I was reading the Bible with passion and fervor. I had read through the book of Isaiah and I was fresh into reading the book of Jeremiah. All of a sudden it occurred to me that the theme of the 98 total pages that I had read so far was the drifting, wandering gaze off of the Power of God!! One of the subtitles in the book of Jeremiah is:

The People Turn Their Back to God.

The next subtitle/page read:

"We Are Free to Roam."

And with my hand and a pen, through my own personal discovery, inference and conclusion I wrote:

"* Theme"

Right there on page 1053, my life-long question was released to me. My life and my world that was consumed with conflict, struggle, confusion, trepidation, anxiety and fear were answered. The premise to my unsettled life was that I was not allowing God's definitive sovereignty to reign in my life. I had been apprehensive to let go and give myself over to the Creator's loving authority; power; influence; control; and command.

The fundamentals of my heart have been changed. It began with my whole- hearted surrender experience. When I turned my back to the former ways of the flesh, the Holy Spirit began to move me onto the course that God my Creator had planned for me from the beginning. Jesus Christ continues to be my Savior and close personal friend! He continues to encourage me, through faith, to press forward onto an abundantly blessed life!

Peace in Heartbreak

Relative to me, the days that lay before me in the year of 2013 continued to produce excruciating circumstances. The horrid events were beyond anything imaginable in my worst nightmare. Contrary to my old behavior, however I felt a peace that the world could never have given me. Because I was ingesting and memorizing God's Word through the Bible; surrounding me with Godly people for support and encouragement; communicating and listening with the Savior through prayer; and worshipping through song, God of the Universe equipped me for what would happen in the near future.

Philippians 4:7 "And the peace of God, which surpasses all comprehension, shall guard your hearts and your minds in Christ Jesus."
The New American Standard Bible

By the month of April it had occurred to me that the year was not even half way completed! I had resolved that each day thereafter I would get up; consciously tip-toe "into" the date on the calendar day and then brace myself for the worst. However, through those dark shrouds of my life I was forced to recognize the bright sun rays of blessings penetrating my soul. A shameful self discovery uncovered how distorted my outlook on life had become. Critical life applications were dismissed and taken for granted so unthankfully. I was bestowed blessings beyond any human comprehension and I was extraordinarily fortunate to be employed by a job I loved passionately. My teaching profession allowed me to pour myself into tiny young souls residing in my own classroom each day. The throbbing pain from my heart instantaneously dissolved and disappeared when I was able to lay my eyes on my students lined up for the day! My God; my Personal Physician replaced that old tattered broken-down heart of mine for a moment and filled it with unbelievable joyfulness. That school year became actively alive and perhaps certain needs of those particular second grade students were filled. I became fueled with intensive, non-stop animation. We laughed and learned entirely throughout the school day. I worked a little bit harder to divert the dreadful thoughts from the circumstances of my life. I was lead to rejuvenated hands-on science experiments and apply substantial educational pedagogies thoughtfully into the curriculum subjects. God helped me control the volume of success in the institution of education while the circumstances in my life were out of control around me.

One particular day late into April, we were celebrating Earth Day. As that Monday school day was winding down I answered a phone call from my husband. I heard these words: "I am calling you because I have just been fired from my job. I have a short-window of opportunity to call you because my cellphone service will be cut off soon." After 15 years of passionate, successful, dedication to his associates and loyalty to this particular service company, his occupation was severed. The luxury of working in America with all its benefits vanished. This included his income; banked-retirement package; affordable insurance premiums; capital gain investments and bonus incentives. Several and all high-end technology communication devises were disengaged and taken away. The oddities of a company vehicle to be used personally; a gas card; full service vehicle repair and access to expensive tools disappeared after lunch on that fateful Monday.

I felt my soul fall gracefully into the arms of Jesus. Directly on that spot where I was standing, close to the 'book return box' in the school library, I envisioned God handing Jesus His own personal blanket made from the feathers of His precious eagles to cover me with Jesus' right hand. That blanket of peace warmly sheltered me as I traversed home along the same long stretch of freeway that

I surrendered my entire being to the Deity of God the Father. The same route in which He clearly told me, "It is not going to be easy." Reality hit me when I turned into the driveway and glanced at the *Home for Sale* sign posted in our yard. Yet still, I was numb-fully at peace. I walked into the front door and walked toward our bedroom. I observed Samuel asleep on our bed and kept walking out the back door as my phone was ringing. Outside I answered the phone to hear these words: "Your home just sold." When I was finished with the phone call, I immediately responded to a knock on our front door. Our brand new friend, who happened to be our neighbor…who happened to be an outstanding pastor at a church we just visited …was standing at our door asking to minister with Samuel. I only ate dinner that night because the pastor insisted on serving us a meal. When I returned home, my heart dropped to the floor in worry and concern. Thankfully I fell asleep immediately. I wasn't alone; Jesus drew me into the comfort of His right hand.

"It's Not Going to Be Easy." God

Eight days later on Tuesday April 30th at the very end of the school day, the phone on my desk rang. The students were loud at dismissal time; the phone was outdated and disconnected several times and the connection was crackled and breaking up. Through the loud clamor I could barely understand what my husband was saying over the phone yet I knew it was something terrible about my oldest daughter. My husband Sam was frustrated and talked quickly:

"Rachel has been in a serious car accident and there is already one person reported dead."

My oldest daughter, Rachel was employed as a manager at a beautiful senior apartment community whose residence were 55 years of age or older. Most were enjoying life as retirees and the apartment complex provided extra amenities to ensure a more carefree way of life! Rachel lovingly connected with the residence that came into the office and she had developed friendships with most of them. On this particular day, one of the managers was home sick and was unable to transport 5 residences whom wished to play card games with other friends at another facility. A young female employee volunteered to drive the small passenger transport bus containing four ladies and one gentleman ages 68-84. When the employee returned to the office, she went out to eat lunch. Her lunch was running longer than expected and it was nearing the time for the residences to be picked up and brought back to their apartments. Rachel volunteered to drive the bus to pick them up. The road back to the apartment complex was a beautifully tree-lined, narrow rural road. It was a clear, warm mid-afternoon day with a few sprinkling of clouds overhead. Rachel spotted a maroon colored sport -utility vehicle veering over the center-line into her lane. She thought this to be very odd and assumed the driver might make its correction and navigate away from heading straight toward her. When the driver did not respond, Rachel compressed her hand long and hard into the horn of the steering wheel. Within fractions of seconds Rachel knew instantly that the impending doom would not be avoided. With both hands now,

"It's Not Going to Be Easy." God

Rachel steered the passenger bus away from the on-coming SUV. The unresponsive driver slammed uncompromising and relentlessly head on into the side of the bus. The force of the impact sent the bus on its side and caused it to slide 80 feet. Its final resting spot was in a shallow grassy ditch, narrowly missing a barbwire fence.

An eerie echo of quietness filled the interior of the passenger bus with its stunned, dazed, and shocked occupants. A distant faint ringing began to emerge deep within Rachel's ears alerting her jogged and fuzzy brain. The electrical impulses began to regenerate and resume her back to the surface of reality and reason. Within milliseconds she was back into the realism of the traumatic events that had just occurred. Rachel grabbed her arms to check to see if she was alive and to bring her mind out of the fog of disbelief. She had to command her mind to follow directions as her body refused to move from the absolute bewildered. She forcefully unstrapped the seatbelt that was holding her in mid-air on the side of her body. She fell with a thud and then turned her head to the bloodshed and carnage behind her. Rachel continued to instruct her brain as she assessed the disbelief before her eyes and the now screams and moaning filling her ears. A man near the back of the bus was hanging in a strange precariously way dangling from his shoulder and lap seat belt. A large woman was crying in pain and gasping for help as her seatbelt was strangulating the circulation of her abdomen causing intensive pain. Oddly, the passenger van had just been thoroughly inspected and the first aid kit contained a seat-belt cutting devise. Rachel fumbled for it; nervously sawed the seat belt and freed the first victim. Another female passenger became angry as she was unable to move. Yet, Janice lay motionless. The only sign of life was a faint and weak moan. Rachel quietly called for her. She talked to her and used words to comfort her. She was in critical and serious condition clinging to life.

Janice was only 74 years of age. She was not the youngest person on the senior bus but her spirit proved otherwise. She could have easily driven herself to the center yet choose

"It's Not Going to Be Easy." God

to occupy the fifth seat in the company of her friends in the bus. The chance to miss out on any of the fun, fellowship or socializing with her friends from that afternoon would have been unthinkable for her. Her character was full of life, love and laughter and she made the others feel young and vivacious! They had had an absolute wonderful afternoon; care-free and entertained. In an instant, however, life for all of them had changed.

On that fateful Tuesday in April at 1:25 p.m. on that skinny, wooded, tiny rural road a 68 year old man was returning home from a physical exam after an operative follow-up doctor's appointment. He had had a major heart procedure done only five days prior. While he was driving in his vehicle, without warning and instantaneously he had a massive heart attack and died. His SUV drifted and swerved into the opposite lane of traffic colliding with the retirement bus. Two witnesses called 911. There were two emergency helicopters that landed and three ambulances that were dispatched to the horrific scene. All emergency vehicles from the small, close-knit community were dispatched. Several firemen had to use a chain saw to cut a 'door' out of a portion of the roof from the bus. Rachel, who did not have life-threatening injuries, remained on the floor near the driver's seat. She was the last to be extracted from the mangled bus. The emergency crew gave words of comfort from the outside of the front windshield now resting on the road. And because Rachel is a Born-Again Believer of Christ Jesus, God dispatched several angels of His own to comfort her inside the bus. However, she had to witness sights and sounds that no human should have to process. Directly behind the seat where she had been driving was where Janice had been sitting. Janice took the full impact of the collision and her foot had been severed from her body. She passed away from this life while being transported by a helicopter in route to the hospital. My daughter, Rachel had to take full impacts from other sources on that horrible late April day. Her impacts are long-lasting yet she doesn't face this world alone. Her Heavenly Father promises to be with her wherever she goes.

The accident reached the public very quickly. It was a high profile news report. Live news coverage was dispatched to the place of the accident and while on air the bus was lifted upright on its wheels. A representative from the urban newspaper reported an interview with the Chief of Police from the rural area:

> "'[Janice] was a personal friend who once made cookies for the police department. It has been a huge blow to the community', B. Kidd said. '[Creekbend] Villas is a tight-knit and large community', said Kidd. 'Everyone is grieving there. We will do all we can but it's going to be tough for them.' " Austin American Statesman email 05/2013

The report was released to the public instantly on social media. The story was segmented into the evening, late and morning news. People who knew Janice were interviewed. Searching for my own answers, I spoke to any and all who were there to help on the scene of the accident aftermath. Their stories never deferred from the facts that Rachel's decisions in handling the head on collision spared lives including hers. I also made note of how Rachel handled the horrific event afterward. In her grief and suffering she could have wavered from her faith in God, yet she never did. She never asked why this happened; she never rebuked her Savior nor did she blame God for what had happened. She depends deeply and personally on God. She continues to work through all the 'head on' events after the accident, yet she does not do it alone. She clutches to her faith; her belief and promises of her personal relationship with a Living God.

Closing Doors

The month of April was behind our family and we were all glad to close the door on that month and the ones before it. The bus accident was still fresh from the recovery of grief and the days of despondency. As a family unit, we were bent down but we were not broken. We were stretched but not shattered. We all picked up the pieces of humanity and continued with our lives. We had been knocked down but we found a way to stand up and wobble back into the existence of daily routines. It was a firsthand account and a reminder of the misfortunes of a fallen world. However, we were a sanctified family of believers. We all made individual choices to accept Jesus Christ as our Lord and Savior. We believe in a God Whom created the world and know that He gives and takes away. We have faith in Jesus Christ, His Only

Begotten Son to guide and comfort us in good times and bad. And we feel, hear and allow the prompting and convictions of the Holy Spirit.

> Jesus said, "For God so loved the world, that He gave His only begotten Son, that whoever believes in Him should not perish, but have eternal life." John 3:16
> The New American Standard Bible

Rachel was able to return back to work but more outstanding than that Rachel was willing to go back to work. Strength and bravery started with getting behind the wheel of a vehicle and then to position herself behind a desk in an office at the same location associated with death and calamity. In addition, a new predisposition resonated at her job now. A bridge was formed conjoining her career and deep personal pain; a connection by heartbreak and tragedy. The commitment to her job came with a cost as she had to relive the surreal reminder of the dreadful memory. Samuel had been let go from his job and was unemployed. He was available if Rachel needed

"It's Not Going to Be Easy." God

him but in the meantime he packed up all of our belongings from the home we loved and lived in for over 10 years.

Our adorable home was located on 3 ½ acres filled with trees and hills. A quiet little creek carved its way through the woods at the base of one of the hills. The land was teaming with wildlife such as deer, rabbits, squirrels, critters and birds. The fondest of memories were formed from that house of over 10 years and were the pinnacle of our life. That home possesses the reminiscences of enjoying our grown daughters as young adults. It afforded Samuel and I time to work on the land for improvements. We traveled more during that time yet couldn't wait to resume our lives on our little compound. Three out of our four grandchildren were born when we were in that home and provided a grandparent's wonderland! It was a place where my family gathered for several occasions such as family photo's; birthdays; graduations and company parties. It served as an entertainment 'summit' for Christmas gatherings; Thanksgiving Day Feasts and Easter egg hunts. We played outside; built bon-fires; camped with tents; took exploration hikes; rode on 4-wheelers and had hay rides. We had a tree swing; a deck overlooking the creek; a barn; a vegetable garden and so much more. In addition, we had neighbors close enough to walk to their home. It was so comforting to have them in that wide open countryside where nothing was close or convenient. Our neighbors decided to adopt two teenage girls from an orphanage located in Ukraine. Samuel and I formed a bond with the girls almost immediately. We knew what it was like to raise teenage girls and offered time and energy to help assimilate them into the American culture. We enjoyed their company so much that our home was open to them anytime. We spent many nights watching movies and eating popcorn. We spurred each other on to cook, bake and create crafts. Samuel and I were given the gift of having a life-time friendship with these two young ladies from a faraway land. Both Sam and I were in our 40's and life just seemed to have come together for us and we were amply happy.

Our happiness however spilled over into forming friendships that we were not equipped to handle in our life. Samuel and I were so consumed with the appeal of our new fun-loving friends that we tossed God's direction for our life aside and carelessly rejected the warning signals around us. We were reckless with the thick veil of sin covering our life that we never anticipated the manifestation of a sleeping-giant in our lives. Deep within our soul a horrid casket of death was exhumed when we began to allow alcohol to flow freely through our home. "Happiness" came with a price and it is what the Bible refers to as folly and foolishness. Even worse we declared ourselves 'living under the grace of God' yet God would not be tested by us and we found ourselves with serious alcohol consumption issues. Oddly enough, we had commanded a strong wall of protection around our home and heart when we were young zealot Christians. There was no desire for alcohol to enter our home. Yet now as I reflect on the past I can see the cracks in the foundation of our home that allowed the evil one to trickle into our life. Our

Godly fortress with foundational boundaries was not maintained and began to fracture around us. Eventually our severe alcohol consumption spilled over onto the streets of our personal and professional life. It never even crossed our path or entered our minds that alcohol would devour us into the sink-hole of torment. The lack of security in ourselves that Christ Jesus could have filled for us if we applied knowledge had us cave into anyone and anything. Samuel and I are passionate people. We love people and God will use us in a powerful way someday to use that character in us. But unchecked we fell into a luring trap of loving people just as they are to the extent of death and destruction.

The massive burden of sin that we had heaped on ourselves weighed us down so deeply that we sank into a trench of anguish. God took mercy on us and we began to crawl out of the pit that we had thrust ourselves into. We temporarily stopped climbing out of the pit for a brief reprieve the very last day of May. I woke up for the very last time in our empty home. And I suppose I was indifferent because the last year there did not in any way resemble the once blessed life that was thriving from this empty home that was void of furniture and life. I drove the familiar route to work for the last day of the school year. I entered the classroom where it would be the last day with the group of students who provided sanctions from my internal pain and external calamity. At the end of the day, my students and I embraced; said goodbye to another school year and welcome the first days of summer. I waved goodbye to the children on the bus and then entered my car for the last drive to my old home. I drove up to an empty house with only remnants of only memories. My youngest daughter was already inside beginning to clean.

I watched Libby on her hands and knees cleaning and I could not believe that God blessed us with this young lady. She was married now with two very small children. She had been battered the worst over the demise of our marriage and the gaping wounds of our alcohol consumption. She had had a front row seat to witness the campaign of obliteration of sin; the battleground of spiritual warfare. It was the battle we entered when God wanted us for His Own Army yet we joined the conflict of sin. Libby didn't know it but not only was she cleaning the empty house for the new owners, she was symbolically washing my filthy feet as Jesus did with His disciples.

> "If I then, the Lord and the Teacher, washed your feet, you also ought to wash one another's feet." John 13:14
> The New American Standard Bible

We had inflicted pain and fear on a caring daughter whose parents were no longer the ones that had raised her as a young child. Libby became a vessel of salvation for me. She could have ignored our troubled life and abandoned us in our pit of disparity. But Libby dressed in garments of Holiness came humbly to serve and honor me in the depth of despair and the unknown. Libby walks upright and daily with God and she lives consciously in God's will. She humbly bowed down low to the filth of myself; my feet and helped picked me up to the place God wanted me to be. We had become unrecognizable as her parents. She watched in horror and endured a heartbreaking witness to the sin that entered our lives. She is a warrior that took many hits to her heart yet found the strength to humbly serve her parents who were reduced to rubble. She valiantly approached us head on to try to ward us away from the sinful path we were headed on to no avail. I think about those times in disbelief and wonder what it is about the human heart to have turned so drastically away from our faith? Because of my new walk with God I look deeper; closely; tighter; and in-depth into each word, verse, story and message of the Bible. I spread out an array of research books connecting the pieces and matching the living words with my human understanding in the day. The word says that God's words are there to uncover the mystery of His messages.

> I Corinthians 2:7-8 "but we speak God's wisdom in a mystery, the hidden *wisdom*, which God predestined before the ages to our glory; the wisdom which none of the rulers of the age has understood; for

> if they had understood it, they would not have crucified the Lord of glory;"
> The New American Standard Bible

I began to see that God's initial desire was to fellowship with His Created in a perfect world. Satan the tempter first started with the fall as Eve was isolated; she was by herself visible to the tree of temptation. Satan perverted God's words and put doubts into Eve's head as she gazed upon the tempting fruit. He was cunning, sneaky, smart and convincing. I was easily convinced to become a part of his sinister plan. I was always the life of the party and the center of attention around a group of friends. Being the life of the party brought me a basket full of the attention I so desperately lacked and needed in my life. It was horrible negative attention but attention just the same. Why I so desperately needed and wanted this attention had to be linked to my early forming heart. My heart was never content until my surrender experience. I had allowed the evil one to begin to cast doubts about the Holy Creator, God. I realize that now my Christian dedication to

God and His Holiness is an uncompromising commitment to His promises. Anything that directs our focus away from Him including doubts is opening a toll road of head on trouble with the appeals of the world eager to lead us further away from God's chosen way. Looking back, I am simply amazed as the shroud of lies layered us by our own hands influenced by Satan. Perhaps we had a 'deep seed' of unworthiness that began to grow as our life moved forward together. The sin in our life was the idols of emptiness that we assumed would be a substantial lifestyle of happiness for us. Equally so, since my surrender experience and after my season of refinement I began to feel so much better. And because I was feeling so happy about my life, I began to seek out several ministries that I could help in with my community. God clearly stated that my only ministry, for now, would be to my marriage and my family. I took heed to His Wise Council. I am fully convinced that the foundation of my marriage has to be unquestionably strong before any type of Christian Ministry is to begin.

My youngest daughter and I cleaned the empty home for over three hours. My body was cleaning as it had been a thousand times before but my mind was detached from the worries ahead of me and the disbelief of where I would be residing when I woke up the next day. Samuel and I would be staying at a worn-out extended stay hotel that accepted our dog. It is not that I was not grateful for a sheltered place to lay our heads but the bewilderment of our life was still unsettled. The consequences of living a non-centered life apart from the Lord was still uncomfortably lurking. We had become strangers in our relationship. There was emotional stress and pain; Samuel seemed different from the constant strain and beatings from the world. After a week at the hotel, we would move into a fifth wheel travel trailer until the Lord led us elsewhere.

It was dark and we finished our cleaning. I drove away from the place where I knew happy memories from the last ten years. I was driving yet to another place where I would witness another chapter closing in my life; the graduation ceremony of the young Ukraine girls that I had loved and cared for over 6 years. I would be witnessing a passage of adulthood into a new world in the new country they now called home. Oddly enough I would be watching the first group of students I had as an elementary teacher when we first moved to the community ten years ago. I made my way to the massive outdoor high school football arena to commence in graduation. It was the first time I sat without any agenda or any responsibilities for a very long time. It was the first time I could allow to process the considerably massive, 'titanic' events only half way through the year; tomorrow would be June. My mind was whisked away by a perfect cool breeze as I sat alone in the huge outdoor football stadium. Tomorrow would represent a new day; a new focus and new direction with my Lord and Savior.

Starting Over

A friend of mine stated one day, "God must have something really enormous for your marriage for Satan to be working so hard to destroy it." That statement confirmed some of my intuitions. I believe that the evil one has had his eyes on our marriage for years.

> "Be of sober *spirit*, be on the alert. Your adversary, the devil, prowls about like a roaring lion, seeking someone to devour." 1 Peter 5:8
> The New American Standard Bible

It all started when Satan swooped into my life almost immediately after I had acted on faith and accepted Jesus Christ as my Personal Savior at the young age of 13. The evil one attached himself to me by way of unresolved issues and sin when I married 8 years later. I was also pregnant when I stood before God during our marriage vows. God wrote my name into the Book of Life waiting for me in Heaven when I became a Christian. However, I was not equipped to handle such strong attacks from the evil one at that age. As a new surrendered believer, I now hold on to the verse:

> "The beginning of wisdom *is:* Acquire wisdom; And with all your acquiring, get understanding." Proverbs 4:7
> The New American Standard Bible

We married quickly and when our daughter was 4 months old, Samuel and I walked forward at a Baptist Church to become members. The Holy Spirit fell upon Samuel and he experienced a radical conversion. Samuel became emotional over a sudden wave of convictions. When he made his way to the altar, he was broken in spirit and he surrendered his life to the Lordship of Jesus Christ. Hours later, on that same day he felt a new awakening in his heart. Days later he had an overwhelming desire to begin a youth camp for troubled teens. And for a few years he was able to help so many young men through Biblical counseling and taught them to love the wilderness of the outdoors. Samuel so desperately wanted a full-time, structured, permanent housing developed for teenagers. He dreamed about this day after day. It is so hard to understand why something so noble to honor God would never come to be. But it is overly clear that God has a different plan for us. Perhaps He saw our future and spared us from irreversible trouble. It is so painful for mere humans to understand when God does not answer our prayers the way we want Him to. This verse directly speaks to me when I am unsure about unanswered prayers:

> John 13:7 "Jesus answered and said to him, ' "What I do you do not realize now, but you shall understand hereafter."'
> The New American Standard Bible

But for our marriage, God the Father has a plan for us. And because we took the matters of our marriage into our own hands we are suffering consequences and delays for our future. Samuel and I did what we knew to do to operate a young family and home but fell short so many times. Our budget was out of control and we were spending out of our means. Samuel felt tremendous pressure to work harder to stay ahead financially. Finally, the pressure was too much and worldly behavior took priority to ease the pain and suffering. Again, Samuel had a strong conviction to restructure our money management. To the dismay of so many people around us, we sold our home and bought a fifth-wheel travel trailer to temporarily live in! Oddly enough, I followed his lead and did not question his decision. But often I battled doubt and would feel insecure about our decision but would remind myself about all the odd places and strange adventures God put His people through in the Bible right before something 'big' would happen. Samuel also reminded me several times about the finances we would save more readily with significantly less expense. We have surrendered together to our Heavenly Father's choosing for us in where we will settle for the last time. It is in His Name and

Authority that it would relent to an obvious vision of God's Glory. Furthermore, it is God's master plan for who I am in Him; from where I started at the beginning of my story. Hand in Hand with our Heavenly Father I would like to live out and see what God the Father had in store for my life all along; something I could never have done myself or anything I could have imagined. Samuel and I have developed a mutual list in our longing for our land and for our future. These desires have never wavered:

- To restructure our life as a ministry to others
- To share our love of the outdoors with others
- To live more independently and cultivate our own wild game, fruits and vegetables
- To live with little debt as we near retirement
- To let our children enjoy a place in nature with their families
- To finalize investment deeds into the hands of our grandchildren to help secure their financial future.

I had a strong sense that the last night at our old home was symbolic to turning our back to a tumultuous past. But in the newness of the next morning would begin a Godly pilgrimage and legacy. It was if the building of our own relationship, etched out by our own doing was erased and God was beginning to redesign a new inheritance with Our Heavenly Father as the lead.

Presently, we live very comfortably in a 360 square feet travel trailer home! Life in it is uncomplicated, so very simple and very little to maintain. We have our trailer home on 44 acres at our best friend's ranch in a very rapidly developing city. Every convenience we need is close at hand, yet we live surrounded by horses; cattle; trees; a river; a lake; a concrete dam with flowing water. We canoe in the lake and hike the river. We bird hunt, fish and host hunting day trips with friends and family. We have a practice shooting range for archery and guns. There are gardens full of tomatoes; onions; potatoes; corn; green beans and an abundance of rose bushes. We give our family 4-wheeler rides; golf cart rides and hay rides. Our grandchildren can sit and play on large heavy machinery such as bulldozers and backhoes. We get to ride horses and watch horse lessons in an arena filled with hay; saddles; cowboys and cowgirls! We get to watch chickens lay on their eggs; baby pigs with their parents and baby horses by their mother's side. In the summer, we swim in a pool with a diving board and a curvy slick slide. There is a full size baseball field where community teams come to practice. There is a long concrete driveway lined with trees to safely ride bikes together. The entrance to the ranch has a stately and regal white iron fence stating its place of importance! The lengthy, solid driveway is lined with a charming picturesque white fence dividing the horse pastures from the drive. To the left I gawk at a trailer we call our home yet to the right I gaze at the surrounding land full of God's glory. Yet one day I climbed on top of the fence and looked up to Heaven. I had felt led to stop what I was doing in the middle of a very busy day. I stared as far as I could see over the stunning simple beauty of the land God created for us to enjoy; the horses, their pasture and the neighbors farm land. It was a quiet moment with my Heavenly Father and I was completely at peace. In the stillness of that short time, He impressed on my heart a glimpse of heaven. Not only did I have a thought in my mind but I had a feeling as well. I felt as if He was saying, "If you think this small piece of land is overwhelmingly beautiful, simple and peaceful just wait for what is ahead in the future for your eternal heavenly home!"

Beautiful Ugly

In this very moment the ranch is gorgeous and magnificent yet there are periodic stacks of junk and garbage. The 44 acre ranch takes an enormous amount of work and up-keep every hour of every single day. It is overwhelmed with up keep, repairs and never ending maintenance. There are places of neglect and piles of trash; heavy equipment and old cars. There are power lines running through the property and heaps of horse manure. In the beginning stages of our move into the trailer and onto the ranch, I was very despondent. There were too many intensive changes for me at times. I was overwhelmed with deep, aching, heart-breaking days of weeping. I would look around and only see the masses of rubbish. One day, there was nothing left of me. I looked around in disbelief and sick to my stomach from the fall-out of drastic changes. I had nowhere but on my knees, face down and prayers lifting up to Him. I asked God to change my view and to help me see my new living arrangements differently in my mind and in my heart. I asked Him if He would be generous enough to let me love the new place. I forced myself to get up and to get moving; to start embracing the surroundings around me. God, my Father gave me an overwhelming fondness of the ranch almost immediately! It started one day when I walked into an old, wooden horse barn and the smell alone brought back early fond childhood memories of my grandparents hay barn. As children we actually swung from and rope and dropped into a pile of hay just like old TV shows! My heart leapt as I began to explore the barn and kiss the horses noses peering out from their stables! It was dusty and dark. I began to smooth out the ruffled disheveled dirt in the hallway of the barn with a garden rake. While I was physically working, my mind was overwhelmed with thoughts of God and my new relationship with Him. He impressed on me that every day is a new day; that He alone is able to 'rake' my ruffled heart clean and new; smooth and level; clean and fresh. The world had a strong hold on me making my heart messy, crumpled and furrowed. God the Father showed me in that exact moment how much He tends to me, loves me and takes care of me. Almost every day I am reminded of yet another quiet, alone time with my Best Friend; the Lord Jesus Christ and the moving of the Holy Spirit.

    Life is beautiful and ugly. God knew all along the impressions that it would take to move my heart in order that I would surrender my all to Him. He also knew how I learn and what it would take to change me. I am reminded everyday of how life can be beautiful and ugly; glorious and dark. I know both in my heart and where I am currently residing. My life has been filled with beauty and blessings. It has been so full of fun, love, laughter and adventures. Before my surrender experience though, my heart would automatically and eventually default into a shroud of deep heavy gloom. And to make matters worse, I used a patchwork of worldly techniques to cover

"It's Not Going to Be Easy." God

so much unhappiness. Living life void of my Heavenly Father's direction caused me to sink deeper and deeper into misery. I finally relinquished, let go, gave up control and fell into faith. I wanted no part of my ways and devices anymore. I was miserable and exhausted. And I also knew deep down that God had a rich life waiting for me. My heart has changed. There is nothing on this earth that could have done that but the One Who Created me. When I surrendered, I heard God say, "Are you sure?" and "It's not going to be easy." I was sure then and I am sure now. It has not been easy and life will still be full of difficulties. I am, however finally at peace living now how God intended me to be.

CPSIA information can be obtained
at www.ICGtesting.com
Printed in the USA
FSOW01n2140080615
7737FS